getting CRAFTY

KNOT PROJECTS

WRITTEN BY

DANA MEACHEN RAU

45TH PARALLEL PRESS

Published in the United States of America by Cherry Lake Publishing Group
Ann Arbor, Michigan
www.cherrylakepublishing.com

Reading Adviser: Beth Walker Gambro, MS, Ed., Reading Consultant, Yorkville, IL
Illustrator: Ashley Dugan
Book Designer: Felicia Macheske

Photo Credits: © vystekimages/Shutterstock, 4; © Murzina Elena Sergeevna/Shutterstock, 5; © yarmrtsnk/Shutterstock, 6; © areetham/Shutterstock, 7; © Therede/Dreamstime.com, 9

45th Parallel Press is an imprint of Cherry Lake Publishing Group.

Library of Congress Cataloging-in-Publication Data

Names: Rau, Dana Meachen, 1971- author. | Dugan, Ashley, illustrator.
Title: Knot projects / written by Dana Meachen Rau ; illustrated by Ashley Dugan.
Description: Ann Arbor, Michigan : Cherry Lake Publishing, [2023] | Series: Getting crafty | Includes
    bibliographical references and index. | Audience: Grades 4-6 | Summary: "Why knot get crafty
    and explore your creative side? Learn new skills and discover the many ways to tie knots to
    create survival bracelets, yarn belts, and more! Book includes an introduction and history on
    knots. It also includes several projects with easy-to-follow step-by-step instructions and
    illustrations. Book is developed to aid struggling and reluctant readers with engaging content,
    carefully chosen vocabulary, and simple sentences. Includes table of contents, glossary, index,
    sidebars, and author biographies"—Provided by publisher.
Identifiers: LCCN 2022041804 | ISBN 9781668920626 (paperback) | ISBN 9781668919606 (hardcover)
    | ISBN 9781668923283 (pdf) | ISBN 9781668921951 (ebook)
Subjects: LCSH: Knots and splices—Juvenile literature. | Ropework—Juvenile literature.
Classification: LCC TT840.R66 R38 2023 | DDC 746.42/2—dc23/eng/20220902
LC record available at https://lccn.loc.gov/2022041804

Cherry Lake Publishing Group would like to acknowledge the work of the Partnership for 21st
Century Learning, a Network of Battelle for Kids. Please visit *http://www.battelleforkids.org/
networks/p21* for more information.

Printed in the United States of America
Corporate Graphics

TABLE of CONTENTS

WHY KNOT?

Knots are useful. Boaters and fishermen use knots. They tie down sails or pull in lobsters. Rock climbers use knots. They keep themselves safe while climbing. Search-and-rescue teams know all sorts of knots. So do campers, soldiers, and farmers. Knitters and crocheters use knots. They make sweaters and blankets. Doctors use knots. They make stitches.

You probably tie knots every day. Need proof? Look at your shoes. A knot probably holds your laces in place! Do you hike or boat or rock climb? You probably know many other types of knots.

Knots can also be pretty. You can use them to make jewelry or belts. You can use them to make key chains. Even works of art. So try some of the knotting crafts in this book. Why knot? It's fun!

KNOT HiSTORY

Knots have probably been around for a long time. As long as people have needed to lift, pull, or attach things. Ancient people used knots. They make tools such as arrows, **snares**, and nets. They used these to catch animals for food. They used knots to pull stones for building. They built things like the Pyramids and Stonehenge.

Ancient knots were **practical**. They were artistic, too. Sailors used knots to tie down sails and make hammocks. In South America, the Incas knotted cords called quipus. Quipus kept track of important numbers. Chinese knots and Celtic knots are works of art.

Many fabric arts use knots. Knitting is a way of making knots on two long needles. Crocheting creates knots using a hook. Macramé is an art form that uses simple knots to make amazing creations.

You can make some amazing knot creations of your own!

BASIC SUPPLIES

You don't need many supplies to make knots. But you'll need plenty of cord. That's important.

TYPES OF CORD

Embroidery floss is made of thin strands of thread. It is cheap. It comes in every color you can imagine. Use this for making friendship bracelets.

Paracord is a nylon cord used for parachute lines. Its smooth surface is easy to tie. It creates a nice look for decorative projects.

Hemp cord has a rough, natural look. You can buy it in its natural brown color. It also comes dyed in other colors.

You can find these cords at craft and sewing stores. They also have other types of cord made of silk, leather, cotton, plastic, and elastic!

OTHER SUPPLIES

A knotting board is made of a piece of cardboard and a binder clip. The board is about the size of a notebook. It forms a flat work surface. The clip holds your work in place.

You will also need scissors for cutting cord. You'll need a tape measure for measuring cord. You'll need a straight pin to help you take out knots if you make a mistake.

If you're making bracelets and belts, you will need clasps. Clasps can be found in craft stores. They come in many types. There are spring rings, lobster claws, magnetic clasps, D-rings, and slide-release buckles.

You might also need index cards, beads, and sticks. And keep a pencil and paper handy to sketch ideas, draw patterns, or keep track of rows.

SAFETY TIP!

Paracord unravels when you cut it. The ends need to be burned with matches or a lighter. Melting it forms a seal. Do not use matches yourself. ASK AN ADULT TO HELP with this part of the paracord bracelet project (see page 24).

BASIC KNOTS and ENDS

LARK'S HEAD KNOT

1. You will need one cord. Fold it in half. Make a loop.

2. Place the loop over the top of a rod or some other object.

3. Thread the loose ends through the loop. Pull tight.

OVERHAND KNOT

1. Make a loop so that the working end lays over the rest of the cord. The working end is the end of the cord that you are tying into knots.

2. Tuck the working end into the loop from back to front. Pull on both ends to tighten.

HALF HITCH KNOT

1. You will need two cords. One cord is the base cord. The other is the tying cord.

2. Place the tying cord over the base cord to form a loop. If you want to work toward the right, the loop needs to be on the left side of the base cord. If you want to work toward the left, the loop needs to be on the right side of the base cord.

3. Tuck the working end of the tying cord under the base cord and up through the loop.

4. Holding the base cord tight, pull on the tying cord so that the knot you've created travels up the base cord to the top. This is a single half hitch. The nub you've created should be the color of the tying cord. If it isn't, you may not have held the base cord tight enough.

5. Repeat steps 2 and 3. You now have a double half hitch knot.

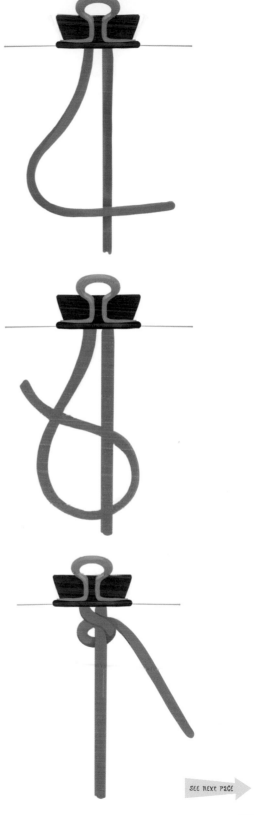

SEE NEXT PAGE

SQUARE KNOT

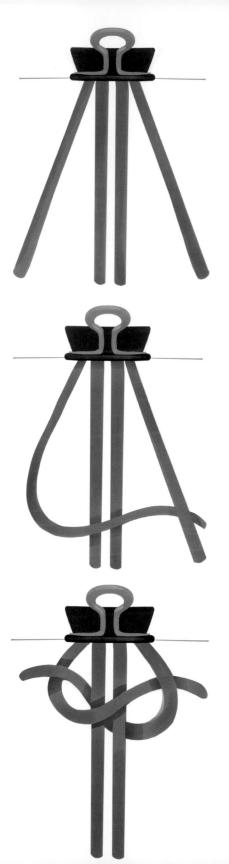

1. You will need four cords. The two center cords are the base cords. The two outer cords are the tying cords.

2. Place the left tying cord over the base cords to make a loop on the left side. Place the right tying cord over the left tying cord.

3. Tuck the working end of the right tying cord under the base cords and up through the loop. Pull tightly on both tying cords. You now have a half knot.

4. Place the left tying cord under the base cords to make a loop on the left side. Place the right tying cord under the left tying cord.

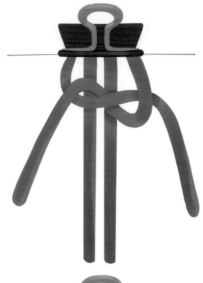

5. Tuck the working end of the right tying cord over the base cords and down through the loop.

6. Pull tightly on both tying cords. You now have a square knot.

SEE NEXT PAGE

TYING THE ENDS

There are a few different ways to end a knot project, especially for bracelets.

You can tie the ends of the cords with two overhand knots around your wrist. Trim off the excess cord. This is best for a bracelet that you don't need to take off.

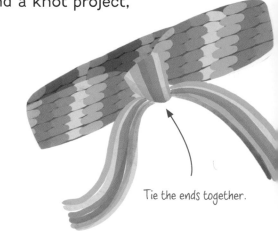

Tie the ends together.

You can start with a loop at the beginning of your bracelet. When you reach the end, separate the strands into two sections and knot them together. Trim off the excess cord. Loosely tie and untie these strands around the loop to put on and take off your bracelet.

You can add a metal clasp. Clasps have two parts: a ring and the clasp. Connect the ring to the strands at the beginning of your bracelet with a lark's head knot. Use an overhand knot to attach the strands at the end to the clasp. Trim any extra cord.

A metal clasp and ring connect this bracelet

MEASURING TIPS

When working with embroidery floss:

Making a six- or eight-strand bracelet? You will need floss that is about six times as long as your wrist. If your wrist measures 7 inches (18 centimeters), multiply that number by six. So each tying cord will need to be 42 inches long (107 cm). If you are going to have a loop or lark's head knot at the beginning of the project, double the measurement for each color of floss. So, for a 7-inch (18 cm) wrist, the floss should be 84 inches (213 cm) long.

When working with paracord:

You will need cord that is about 12 times as long as your wrist. If your wrist measures 6 inches (15 cm), you will need about 72 inches (183 cm) of paracord.

For all types of cord, always add a little extra. That way you don't run out as you work. Did you run out of cord by mistake? Connect a new piece to the old. Use an overhand knot (see page 10).

BRAID BRACELETS

Braiding isn't just for hair. You can braid cords to make cool bracelets, too. Decide how you will clasp or tie your bracelet (see page 14). Now you can start and end your project as needed.

THREE-STRAND BRACELET

You will need three cords of the same length.

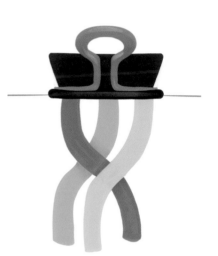

1. Cross the left strand over the middle strand.

2. Cross the right strand over the new middle strand.

3. Continue crossing the outside strands over the middle strand, **alternating** left and right until you reach the end.

FOUR-STRAND BRACELET

You will need two cords of the same length.

1. Loop the middle of one cord over the middle of the other. Think of the four loose ends as **A**, **B**, **C**, and **D**.

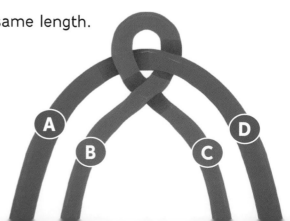

2. Cross **B** over **A** and **C** over **D**.

3. Cross **A** over **D**. Pull on all the cords to tighten.

4. Think of the loose ends from left to right as **A**, **B**, **C**, and **D** again. Repeat steps 2 and 3 until you reach the end.

SEESAW BRACELET

You will need two cords of the same length.

1. Tie a single half hitch knot with the left cord as the tying cord and the right cord as the base cord (see page 11).

2. Tie a single half hitch knot with the right cord as the tying cord and the left cord as the base cord.

3. Continue alternating single half hitch knots on the left and right cords until you reach the end.

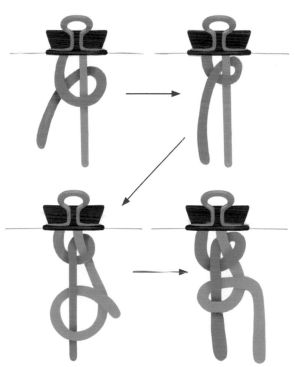

RAINBOW FRIENDSHIP BRACELET

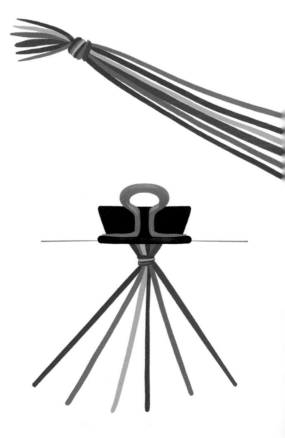

Use all the colors of the rainbow! Make a bracelet you can share with someone you care about.

MATERIALS

- Embroidery floss in red, orange, yellow, green, blue, and purple
- Tape measure
- Scissors
- Knotting board

STEPS

1. Cut the needed length of floss from each color (see measuring tips on page 15). Gather the ends. Tie them in a loose overhand knot. Leave about a 6-inch (15 cm) tail.

2. Clip the strands to your knotting board. Clip above the knot. Arrange them in the order they would be on a rainbow: red, orange, yellow, green, blue, purple.

3. Start on the left. You will be moving toward the right. Red will be your tying cord. Orange will be your base cord. Tie a double half hitch knot (see page 11).

4. Red will be your tying cord again. But this time, yellow will be your base cord. Tie a double half hitch knot. Continue tying double half hitch knots. Use the red tying cord across the green, blue, and purple cords. When you finish, the red strand will be on the right. You have completed a row.

5. Repeat steps 3 and 4 with orange as your tying cord. Then repeat with yellow, green, blue, and purple. Once you have worked all the colors as tying cords, you will have a set of rainbow-colored stripes.

6. Continue making full sets of rainbow stripes. Do this until your bracelet is the right length. Take the bracelet off the board. Untie the top overhand knot. Tie the bracelet ends together on your friend's wrist.

As the bracelet grows longer, you can unclip it from the board. Move it up. Clip it again. This will make it easier to work.

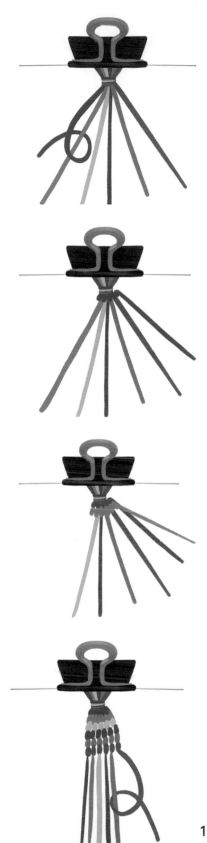

CHEVRON FRIENDSHIP BRACELET

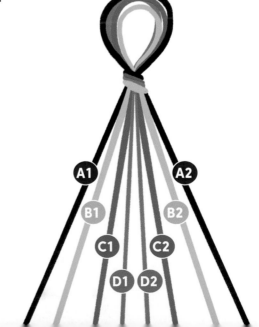

A chevron pattern is made up of V shapes. You will need only four colors for this bracelet. You will be working with eight strands. Decide how you will clasp or tie your bracelet (see page 14). Now you can start and end the project as needed.

MATERIALS
- Embroidery floss in four colors
- Tape measure
- Scissors
- Knotting board

STEPS

1. Cut the needed length of floss from each color (see measuring tips on page 15). Gather your strands. Fold them at the center. Tie them in a tight overhand knot to form a loop. Or attach them to the ring of a clasp.

2. Clip your project to your board. Arrange the strands so their colors are **symmetrical**. You can think of them as colors **A1**, **B1**, **C1**, **D1**, **D2**, **C2**, **B2**, and **A2**.

3. Starting on the left, tie color **A1** toward the right in double half hitch knots across base cords **B1**, **C1**, and **D1**.

4. Starting on the right, tie color **A2** toward the left in doublehalf hitch knots across base cords **B2**, **C2**, and **D2**.

5. Color **A1** and **A2** are now in the center. Double half hitch knot these strands together. You have completed one row.

6. Tie colors **B1** and **B2** from both sides into the center. Then continue with **C** and **D** to complete a full set of colors. Repeat the pattern. Do this until your bracelet is the right length.

Knot the ends or tie on a clasp.

STRIPED YARN BELT

You can use double half hitch knots for many things! Way more than just friendship bracelets. Use thicker cords, like yarn. You can make a colorful belt. Choose your two favorite colors. Make a striped fashion statement!

MATERIALS

- Two 35-foot (11 meters) lengths of medium-weight yarn in color **A**
- Two 35-foot (11 m) lengths of medium-weight yarn in color **B**

- Two D-rings
- Knotting board
- Tape measure
- Scissors

STEPS

1. Gather your strands. Fold them at the center. Attach them to both D-rings with a lark's head knot.

2. Clip the D-rings to your board. Arrange the cords as **A1**, **A2**, **A3**, **A4**, **B1**, **B2**, **B3**, and **B4**.

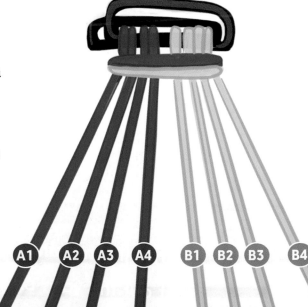

3. Start with color **A1** on the left. Tie double half hitch knots toward the right. Go across all the base cords as you would for the rainbow friendship bracelet project (see pages 18 to 19). Continue with cords **A2**, **A3**, **A4**, **B1**, **B2**, **B3**, and **B4**. You'll see the striped pattern start to form.

4. Continue tying until the belt is the length of your waist. Plus about 8 inches (20 cm). Separate the color **A** and color **B** cords. Tie the four strands of each color in an overhand knot. Trim off the extra. Leave some on the end as **fringe**.

5. To wear the belt, stick the end through both rings. Thread the end back through one ring. Pull to tighten.

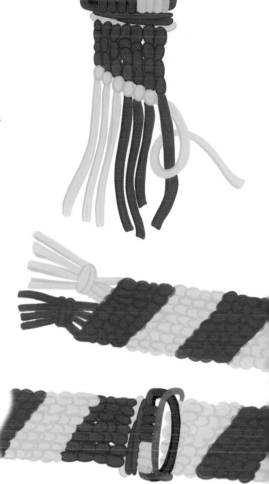

You will be working with very long lengths of yarn in this project. To keep the strands from tangling together, it is helpful to make **bobbins** before you start.

1. Fold an index card in half. Fold it in half again. Cut two slits into the folded edge. One near each end.

2. Slip the end of the yarn into one of the slits. Wrap the yarn around and around the card. Slip the yarn into the other slit to hold it in place.

3. Let out the yarn bit by bit as you work.

PARACORD SURVIVAL BRACELET

Soldiers and campers sometimes wear survival bracelets. They might need cord on their travels. They can unravel their bracelets! Make one for yourself. Stay prepared! (But don't worry—you don't have to unravel this bracelet if you don't want to!)

MATERIALS

- About 10 feet (3 m) of paracord
- Slide-release buckle
- Knotting board
- Tape measure
- Fabric scissors
- Matches

STEPS

1. Slip both ends of the paracord into one half of the slide-release buckle. Go from back to front. Pull them almost all of the way through. Tie a lark's head knot.

2. Slip the ends into the other half of the buckle. Go from front to back. Pull the cords through. Pull until the length between buckles is about the size of your wrist.

3. Attach the buckles together on your wrist. Pull on the loose ends until the bracelet fits well. You don't want it to be too tight. You don't want it too loose. Make sure you can still slip two fingers between the buckle and your wrist.

4. Take off the bracelet. Be careful. You don't want to lose the length. Clip the unknotted buckle end to the top of your board. You should have four strands hanging down. The middle two are tied to the other half of the buckle. The other two are loose.

5. Tie the outer tying cords onto the base cords. Use a square knot (see pages 12 to 13). Pull the ends tight.

6. Continue tying square knots. Tie until you reach the end. Do not tighten the last knot.

7. Flip your bracelet over. You should see the back side. Tuck the two working ends into the last two stitches. Pull everything tight.

8. Use the fabric scissors to trim the ends. Ask an adult to burn the ends. This will keep them from unraveling. Do not try to do this part of the project yourself!

9. Clip it onto your wrist!

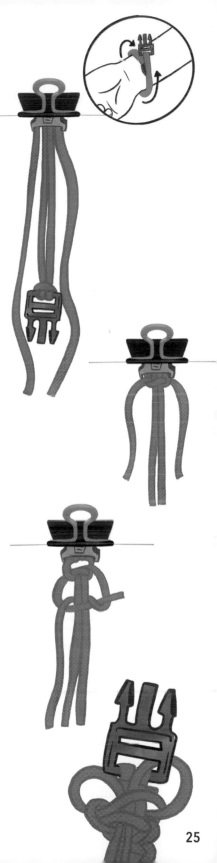

BEADED WALL HANGING

Dress up your walls! Make a beautiful pattern of square knots and beads. Use sticks, hemp cord, and wooden beads. Your project will have a natural look.

MATERIALS

- Ten 9-foot (2.7 m) lengths of hemp cord
- Two 6-inch (15 cm) sticks
- Knotting board
- Wooden beads
- Tape measure
- Scissors
- One 3-foot (0.9 m) length of hemp cord

STEPS

1. Fold each of the 9-foot (2.7 m) cords in half. Tie them to one of the sticks using lark's head knots. Attach the stick to your board with clips.

2. Use the first four cords to tie a square knot (see pages 12 to 13). The second and third strands will be base cords. The first and fourth strands will be tying cords. Continue across all the sets of cords. You will have a row with five square knots.

3. For the next row, you will connect these five sets together with square knots. Starting on the left, use the right tying cord of the first set and the left tying cord of the second set as base cords. Tie a square knot. Continue this across the other sets. You will now have a row with four square knots.

4. Repeat step 2 to make another row with five square knots.

5. Thread a wooden bead onto each set of base cords. Tie a square knot under each bead to hold it in place.

6. Repeat steps 3 to 5—a row of four square knots, a row of five square knots, a row of beads, and a row of five square knots. Continue in this way until your project is the right length.

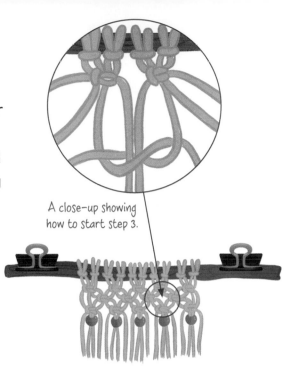

A close-up showing how to start step 3.

SEE NEXT PAGE

7. For the next row, place the base cords in front of the other stick and the tying cords behind it. Tie square knots below the stick across the five sets to hold the stick in place.

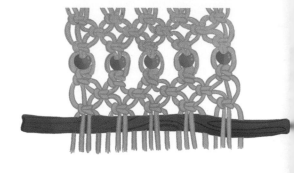

8. For the next row, tie four alternating square knots.

9. For the next row, tie three square knots, then two, and finally just one. You will have created a triangle shape.

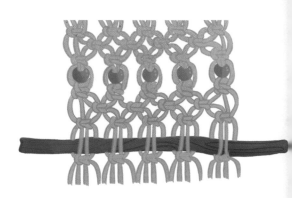

10. Trim the ends to about 4 inches (10 cm) long. Secure each end with an overhand knot.

11. To hang your project, fold the 3-foot (0.9 m) length of cord in half. Attach it to one end of the top stick. Use a lark's head knot. Tie the cord with a seesaw pattern (see page 17). Tie until you reach the right length. Tie the loose ends to the other side of the stick. Use two overhand knots. Trim any extra cord.

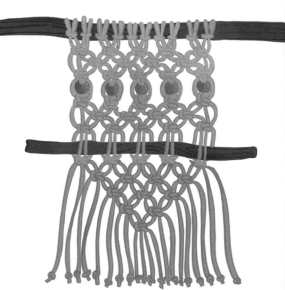

MIX and MATCH IDEAS

You've learned a lot of different knot skills. You've made lots of projects. Now it's time to test new ideas! Mix and match cords, knots, and clasps. Here are some ideas:

- Follow the steps for the paracord bracelet on pages 24 to 25. But make it longer. Make it a dog collar, a belt, or even a leash!

- Try attaching friendship bracelets to key rings! Try this instead of clasps. You can make unique handcrafted key chains.

- Is the natural look of the wall hanging on page 26 not your thing? Jazz it up by using colorful pencils instead of sticks. Use silk cord instead of hemp. And plastic pony beads instead of wooden ones.

- Try the braided bracelet techniques on pages 16 to 17 in your hair!

Think small. Think big! Think any way you want. Follow your ideas and try something new with knots!

GLOSSARY

alternating (AWL-tuhr-nay-ting) going back and forth between two things

bobbins (BAH-buhnz) devices used to hold thread

fringe (FRINJ) loose threads at the edge of an item of clothing

practical (PRAK-ti-kuhl) useful and sensible

snares (SNAIRZ) loops of wire or cord that are used to capture animals

FOR MORE INFORMATION

BOOKS

Pshednovek, Ariela. *Spectacular Friendship Bracelets*. Watertown, MA: Charlesbridge, 2016.

Stetson, Emily. *40 Knots to Know: Hitches, Loops, Bends and Bindings*. Charlotte, VT: Williamson Publishing Company, 2002.

Strutt, Laura. *Arm Candy: Friendship Bracelets to Make and Share*. Hauppauge, NY: Barron's Educational Series, Inc., 2015.

Sundsten, Berndt, and Jan Jäger. *My First Book of Knots*. New York: Skyhorse, 2009.

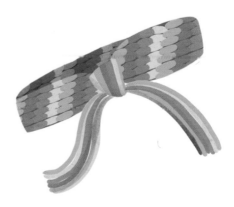

INDEX